pure beauty pure style

Flowers

pure beauty pure style

Flowers

Tricia Guild

Photographs by James Merrell

Text by Elspeth Thompson with Tricia Guild

Quadrille

Contents

Flowers have a language and essence of their own. I have always been touched by the purity and spirit of this language and try to absorb their essence into my life and work. Looking, sensing and trying to understand one of earth's miracles brings further questions and allows me to learn more. As a designer, flowers form a crucial part of my creative process, providing inspiration for patterns and colours. And at home, where I grow them in my gardens both in London and in Italy, flowers are a constant presence around the house, transforming rooms with their beauty, style, warmth and feeling.

The more I learn about flowers, the more I appreciate their purity. They do not need to be displayed in elaborate

Introduction

Tricia Guild

arrangements to be seen at their best. On the contrary, just a few blooms, well chosen and thoughtfully placed, have the power to change the balance of an interior, to create different moods and delight the spirit. Time taken on flowers is never wasted. Selecting, arranging and caring for them is, for me, one of life's most beautiful and rewarding rituals.

These pages are my personal homage to flowers. I hope to share my love of them, my respect for them and some of the creative spirit with which I try to respond to their miraculous colours, shapes and scents. Whether the end result is romantic or rustic, modern, minimal or exotic, the same loving care and fascination lies behind every vase.

City

Flowers bring a city home to life, providing a vital connection with wild nature and the changing seasons. Buying fresh flowers every week from the flower shop or market and bringing them home to arrange around the house is a life-enhancing ritual that gives meaning and joy to urban living. There's no such thing as a 'city flower'. Though it's true that some of the more architectural shapes and strong colours favoured by stylish florists can lend an air of urban sophistication to both period and modern interiors, garden flowers such as peonies and guelder roses can look equally at home. It's more to do with the way that the flowers are used – bringing something of the wit, style and sophistication that makes city life all over the world so alluring and exciting.

At home in London, I change the mood and feel of the rooms with different flowers. There is colour in this sitting room, and fresh flowers can accentuate the colour, contrast or calm the atmosphere. At one end of the room, the bright accent colours of the curtains, cushions and other furnishings have been used in the flowers – a mixture of garden and florist's blooms as gloriously eclectic and unexpected as city life itself. It is creative finding new ways to use classic favourites. Peonies – for some the quintessential country flower – are seldom displayed singly on long stems with architectural alliums or nerines. Or, for a different but equally strong look, cut the cleaned stems to fifteen centimetres and plunge them into a low bowl – the mass of papery petals has a wonderful air of opulence, and on a practical note, the heavy blooms will be less prone to droop.

'I just heard you singing. The words of your song belong to eternity.'

Quach Thoai, *Dahlia*

With their graphic shapes and unexpected colours, dahlias are a natural choice for the urban interior. Here in this modern city loft, they are perfectly complemented by the chunky shapes and rich jewel colours of these glass vases and tea glasses – the posies of blooms given a quirky touch with a few lupin leaves and some spindly stems of white chincherinchees for height. The colours refer back to the fabrics and furnishings in a wonderfully rich layering of pattern on pattern.

Some flowers are famously ephemeral – Icelandic poppies live out their brief but beautiful lives in the space of a few days. It is a joy to watch the fat, hairy buds swell and open, spilling out crinkled papery petals in citrus shades that frill themselves in the warmth. Accentuate the kinks in the stems – keep them long, in a tall glass vase with just one ramrod straight allium or chincherinchee – and let the colours sing out in style against a contrasting plain backdrop.

It is fun to display familiar flowers in a completely new way. Take this mass of half-open daffodils in a plain glass ice

bucket: with stems tightly trussed, no leaves, and laid on the slant, they are suddenly sculptural, modern and urban

– a far cry from Wordsworth's dancing golden clouds. And yet, against the fresh lime-green walls, the intensity of

yellow is like a splash of country sunshine in the heart of the city.

Vintage

Timeless yet contemporary, the vintage look for interiors has never been so fashionable. And there are plenty of flowers that are the perfect complement for treasures and trinkets from times gone by. Roses are a great choice – not the blowsy old-fashioned types, but the tight pointed buds and pristine blooms of candy-pink hybrid teas, with all their associations of 1950s glamour. Camellias, with their glossy leaves and waxy pastel petals, have a movie-star charm, harking back to the 1940s – a single bloom in a small vase could be waiting to be plucked for a corsage on a ball gown. Peonies seem straight from a vintage print, while whorls of ranunculus petals look as if they have been cut from softest silk – don't confine them to vases but use them in other witty and unexpected ways.

'You may break, you may shatter the vase, if you will, but the scent of the roses will hang round it still.'

Thomas Moore, Irish songwriter

Vibrant colour and quirky touches bring the elegant period features of this bedroom to life. Confining the colour scheme to pinks would have been less fun and here, the mass of orange ranunculus – stalks cut short and crammed into a Chinoiserie-style cup and saucer – are a welcome surprise. Decadent details give the room the seductive air of a boudoir. In front of the fire, garlands made from white tuberose, ranunculus and peonies are hung like floral necklaces, while scent – the ultimate seductress – hangs heavy in the air.

Taking its cue from the collection of vintage prints and other framed pictures above the fireplace, the colour scheme for the flowers in this bedroom is an unusual mix of muted mauves, offset with white and fresh lime green. Arranged in sparse, asymmetric posies along the mantelpiece (see also previous page), or singly in tiny clear glass vases just a few centimetres high, Victorian favourites – such as roses, pansies, fritillaries and lily-of-the-valley – are by this means given a fresh contemporary twist.

'A flower is the most eligible object in the world.'

Donita Ferguson

'The blind beauty, the lonely fragrance, the twisted art, the seduction without shame, that we adore and call a flower.'

Donald Culross Peattie

Mixing periods and types of flower keeps things fresh: on a vintage Italian table by the window dark dusky bells of *Fritillaria persica* are paired with white Soloman's seal and apple blossom in a 1950s vase, while pink sweet peas look pretty in a lustre-ware teacup with a single hosta leaf laid alongside. Sweet peas, with their frilled and fragrant petals, have an old-fashioned charm, and the brownish bells of the fritillaries are suffused with Victorian melancholy. But these little arrangements have a wit and grace that brings them right up to date.

As decorative as tasselled vintage bell-pulls, garlands of white hyacinth bells and pale pink roses hang from the chandelier in this ultra-feminine sitting room. Sprays of cherry, pear and hawthorn blossom are fresh and prettily nostalgic alongside peonies, rosebuds and the odd dark-pink primula. Bring branches of spring blossom inside while still in bud; the flowers will soon open in the warmth and fill the room with their fragile, ephemeral beauty – then save tiny sprigs that fall to tuck into smaller vases.

Bearded iris, single white peony, frilled double peony, Soloman's seal and a lacy froth of dill.

Modern

Flowers are neither modern nor old-fashioned in themselves, but some have certain associations. Violets and hydrangeas, for instance, seem to hark back to Victorian times – but surely that's a cue to reinvent them, with minimal styling and contemporary containers. Any flower can look modern if used in the right way. The key lies in keeping things simple. This doesn't mean minimal: some of the following arrangements are actually quite elaborate. But if you are using many different flowers, or many little arrangements, do cut down on colour – just one or two at the most, with possibly a contrasting accent. And it helps to keep the silhouette clear, clean and graphic. Flowers do rise to their setting, of course – and that includes contemporary containers as well as the fabric and furnishings of the room.

There were already accents of red in my London studio, mainly in the collection of contemporary ceramics and Perspex and glass vases. Taking the colour cue from these for the flowers has given this light modern space a heightened energy and vitality. Dahlias in different shades of red, from scarlet to dark crimson, have a stylized graphic quality that looks instantly modern, especially when stripped of their leaves. Rather than mass them in one large bunch, the flowers have been arranged in ones and twos throughout the room.

Proof that you don't have to be minimal to be modern, these pretty garden flowers are arranged in a contemporary style. Massed together, the alliums, iris, wisteria, hyacinths and rosebuds would look countrified and romantic. Instead, they are divided into contrasting shapes and heights and displayed for maximum graphic impact. Alternating erect bearded irises with drooping fronds of wisteria along the mantelpiece is an original touch, as is cutting just one allium head short so it nestles in the top of a vase of taller blooms.

'... Twice dappled

with drizzle and beauty marks, she tilted a bit in her vase

toward my pencil as if she could lift it to write

and tell me the checkered story of all things in bloom...'

James Reiss, *Lily*

This elegant period room has already been given a contemporary feel with wallpaper and furnishings that are a modern take on classical. The flowers take the look further, with a spirited mix of bright pink nerine lilies and peonies, with contrasting green foliage and touches of pale pink and white. Clear glass vases are ranged along the mantelpiece while, on the table, Salviati hand-made vases knit the colours and forms of flowers, foliage and furnishings together. The addition of just one scarlet single peony head throws the scheme pleasantly off-centre.

Romantic

All flowers are romantic. From time immemorial all cultures have used them to say "I love you", to decorate weddings and to mark anniversaries. It is hard to imagine a setting for romance without flowers. Roses, lilies and violets are traditionally thought of as romantic, but individual flowers can form their own more personal associations – for some people it may be bluebells from a long-remembered walk, or the heady, seductive scent of tuberose. Romance is all about mood and atmosphere – soft colours, delicate textures, and the feeling that time and trouble has been taken to create something special. When it comes to flowers this may mean tiny bedside posies of violets, pink-tinged rosebuds in gilded teacups or even delicate garlands of fragrant hyacinth bells. Flowers such as these have the power to open a closed heart.

Many people associate pink with romance, but for me it's the colour blue. The soft textured blue on my bedroom walls has a lot of red in it, making it the perfect foil for mauve flowers such as alliums, delphiniums, hyacinths and sweet peas. Colours and textures are soft and the arrangements informal, with sprays of delphinium buds and half-open alliums as an unusual touch, and garlands of hyacinth bells hung from the ceiling and reflected in mirrors. The furniture is all quite modern, which makes the delicate shapes of the flowers more fragile.

ASSO LA JOIE 1945
DE VIVRE 1948

Skira

palazzo
grassi

'Earth returns
Kisses from sky
In blossoms.'

Anonymous haiku poet

Touches of pale pink soften the series of green-and-white arrangements in this period room. The delicacy of the shapes and colours suggests the dappled light of a woodland in spring, with Soloman's seal and sprays of white blossom reflected gracefully in the mirror behind. On the mantelpiece, the gleam of antique silver augments the charm of vintage vases and unadorned glass. Scent is incredibly romantic, of course, and it only takes a couple of white hyacinths to fill the whole room with their perfume.

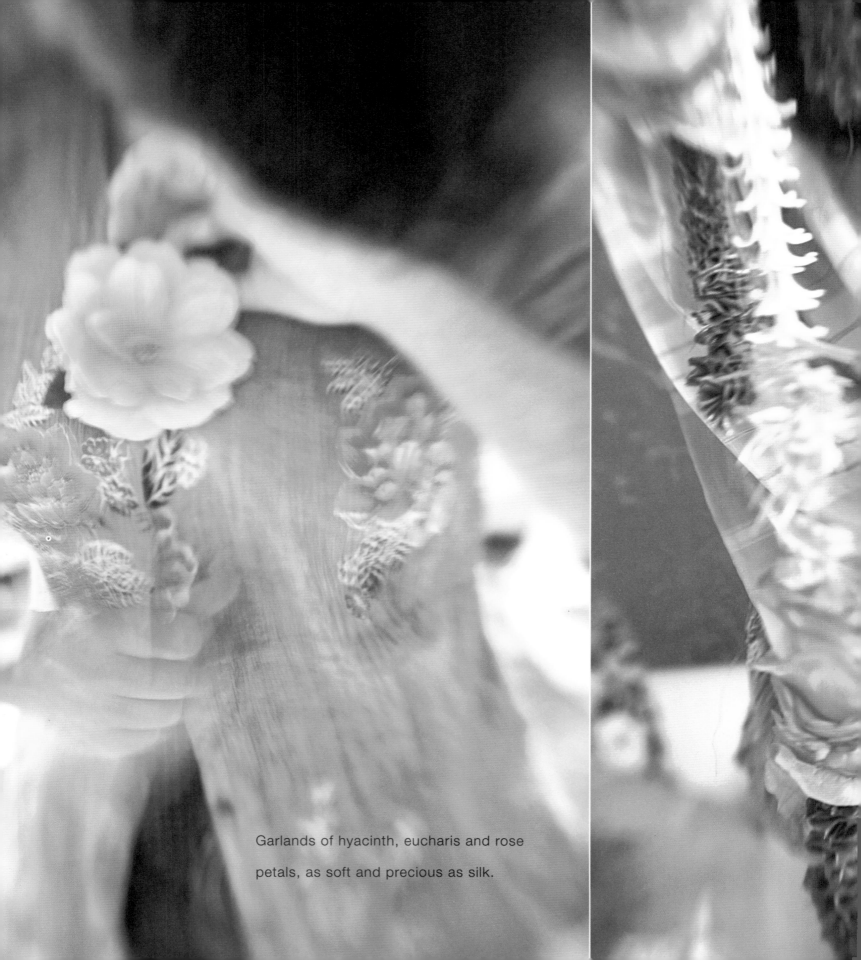

Garlands of hyacinth, eucharis and rose petals, as soft and precious as silk.

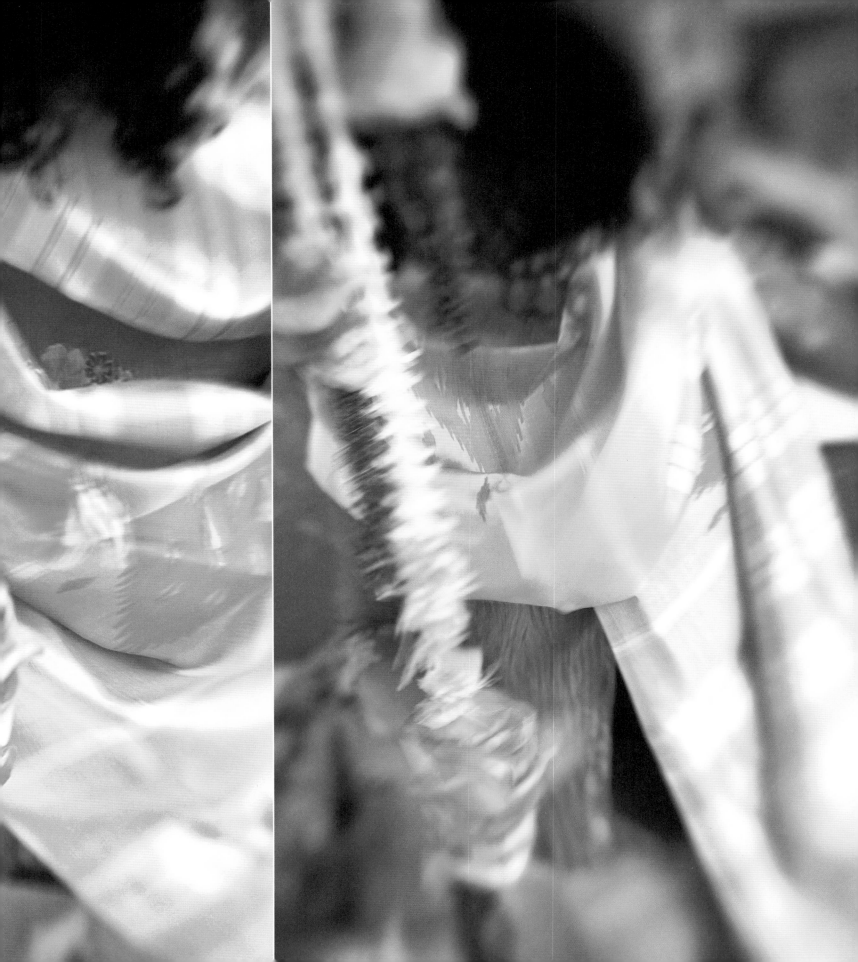

Imagine awakening to these beautiful, yet unassuming offerings beside the bed. Pastel pink peonies are lushly luxurious, along with soft half-open rosebuds and a few parrot tulips striped in delicate pinks and milky greens. Vases are small, in plain or coloured glass, or pretty patterned jugs – a couple of blooms even lie in shallow water on an antique majolica plate. The fragility of the flowers only heightens the romantic mood – they are at their fullest and most lovely, poised on the point of decay. The beauty of this moment cannot last for long.

'Gather ye rosebuds while ye may,
Old Time is still a-flying:
And this same flower that smiles today,
Tomorrow will be dying.'

Robert Herrick, *To the Virgins, to Make Much of Time*

Party

It's easy to buy a big bunch of flowers for a party and leave it at that. But flowers can be used in a multitude of other ways to decorate the whole house in the mood and style of your choice. Wherever you might use paper or other artificial decorations, think of fresh flowers instead. String them in garlands to hang from the ceiling or suspend from ribbons out of doors in a fantastic floral canopy. Tie them to chair backs or attach them to presents. Scatter rose petals on tables or heap them in open bowls. And why use sugared or false flowers on cakes and puddings when real ones are so much more beautiful? Many of the following are ephemeral creations that take time and effort to produce. But their life-enhancing beauty, shared by many, is well worth it.

Fresh flowers can make an attractive alternative to traditional Christmas decorations. Long-lasting flowers such as carnations can be strung in bright garlands (using clear plastic fishing line and lengths of frayed silk fabric) or attached to the branches of a Christmas tree, where the contrast with the deep green needles is fantastic. A daily spray with water keeps them fresh for a good few days.

Country

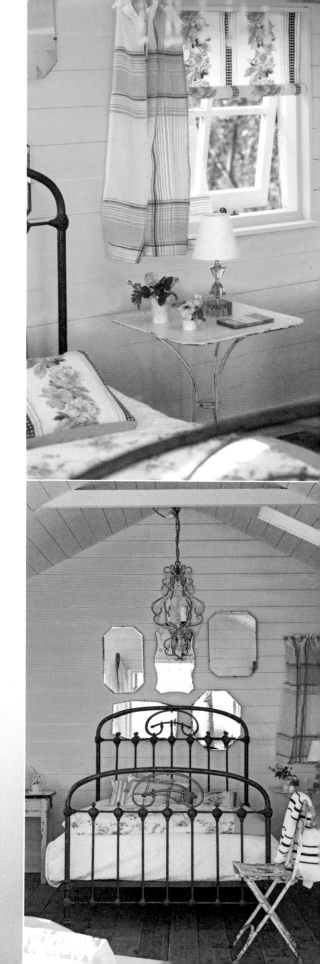

In a country setting, cut flowers need no elaborate arranging or adornment – they are a simple extension of the rural surroundings brought inside the home. Cottage garden favourites such as roses, tulips and ranunculus in pretty pastel colours can be picked fresh from the garden and placed in simple posies on bedsides and windowsills. Smaller blooms such as primroses and pansies, which can often go unnoticed in the garden, can be enjoyed at close quarters in simple uncluttered arrangements in vintage cups and saucers. Take colour cues from faded floral fabrics or the patterns on old china plates. Sprigs of bright green foliage keep the look fresh and the colours uncloying – experiment with lime alchemilla, feathery fennel, tiny chervil and textured primrose leaves to contrast with pastel pinks and mauves.

Traditional mixed bunches of flowers can make a large period room such as this in a French country farmhouse seem fussy and old-fashioned. Instead, this spontaneous mix of peonies, alliums and dahlias in all shades of pink and white are like a breath of fresh country air.

Some stems have been left long, as a nod to the high ceilings and elegant proportions of the room, but a mix of short and tall stems in one vase is a quirky touch that gives the space a modern feel. None of these flowers has particularly attractive foliage, so most has been stripped to leave a strong graphic silhouette. In its place, a few hosta leaves in the same fresh lime green as the cushions and patterned vase weave the whole look together.

Green-and-white flowers in tiny vases transform an antique tray of pretty scent bottles into a charming tableau. Green carnations, dusky hellebores, papery white peonies and – unusally – a spray of fragrant elderflower are tucked into little glass vases and bottles in front of the window, where the sunlight can shine through the fragile leaves and petals. A few little florets even adorn the lovely old lace curtains – touches such as these can make a guest bathroom wonderfully welcoming.

'Flowers leave some of their fragrance in the hand that bestows them.'

Chinese proverb

I love the opulence of guelder roses, their heavy clusters of tiny florets in that unexpected minty green. Native English flowers that can still be found in country hedgerows, they also make wonderful cut flowers. Here in my London bathroom, they bring the fresh beauty of the countryside to a city setting, teamed with other cottage garden flowers such as lilac, bluebells, hellebores, ranunculus and a single delphinium spire. Contemporary containers and the artful asymmetry of the arrangements are what give them a modern, urban twist.

The peony print on this wallpaper is so striking it made sense to bring it to life by filling the room with real flowers in the same rich crimsons, pinks and white. Though often thought of as cottage garden flowers, peonies have an aristocratic and exotic past, and their opulent frilled petals are at home in any setting. All the colour in this elegant

white-panelled room is provided by the flowers and fabric, so it was important to choose flowers that picked out the tones of the furnishings exactly. Ranged on the mantelpiece in antique glass bottles of decreasing size, the lime green leaves of Soloman's seal echo the fresh green of the wallpaper. With its gracefully arching stems and pendant white flowers, this lovely woodland plant should be used more often as a cut flower.

'And they were open like lips, and pouted like lips... Each midnight velvet petal saying touch-touch-touch.'

Sharon Olds, *My Mother's Pansies*

Pansies are so beautiful – I love the way they smile at you. Their beautiful patchwork faces can get lost in crowded arrangements so I like to use them in simple small-scale posies with just a few other garden flowers in shades that complement their colours. Here on this bedroom mantelpiece, just a few selected blooms in old glass bottles look much prettier than one large bunch. The fresh green of scented geranium leaves is the perfect foil for clear pinks and mauves.

Exotic

For centuries, flowers have been our most intense source of colour and beauty, and even in this age of digital imagery and mass production their vibrant shapes and colours still have the power to move and amaze. Flowers play a rich part in the religious rituals and everyday lives of people of many cultures. The ancient temples of India are strung with garlands of fresh marigolds, while cows and elephants wander the streets with flowers around their necks. Buddhist monks hold flowers as the focus of their meditations, while in Bali, tiny, intricate offerings of leaves and flowers are made to the gods at certain times of the day. Unconsciously, we are probably doing something similar ourselves, as we place a flower on a grave, or reverently arrange a vase of blooms on a table or mantelpiece.

Yellow with crimson; scarlet with cerise – bright clashing colours bring some of the exoticism of India to this modern London loft. Flowers, whether fresh, or on fabric or ceramics, provide almost all the colour in this space. Arranged in clustered groups on tables, shelves and trays, they are almost like offerings on little altars. Some of the tiniest arrangements have the strongest impact: dark carnation heads and scattered rose petals in small metal prayer bowls; sprigs of pink sweet pea in a cup; a pile of yellow ranunculus and pink carnations.

Making garlands of fresh flowers is a time-consuming process, but the end result is glorious, so it is definitely worth doing for a party or special celebration. You could even ask friends or family to help – older children love making what are, in essence, grown-up daisy chains. Use cotton or fine fishing line, and take care to thread through the thickest part of the flower or bud. Stored in the fridge overnight, and sprayed regularly with water, they should last a few days, depending on the flowers used.

Carnations are not the most fashionable flowers, but they are due for a revival in the style stakes. They come in beautiful rich colours, and last a long time, which means they are good to use in garlands and other decorations where they will be without water for some time. If you are cutting the heads short to float on water in a shallow bowl, gently tear the green calyx at the back of the flower – this frees the petals and allows them to frill out for a looser, more relaxed look.

Minimal

Flowers have a natural opulence and abundance, but used with care and consideration, they can also be strikingly graphic – even minimal at times. It's all a matter of choosing the appropriate blooms, pairing them with the right containers, and editing colours, shapes and textures down to a minimum. Take time to look at the sculptural forms of different leaves, the intricate geometry of a flower, the subtly repeating patterns in the sequence of its petals. Some flowers have strong architectural stems that can be used to great effect; others a purity of form that needs only a contrasting backdrop to set them off. There are some flowers whose markings have all the intensity of abstract art. Less is often more – though at times a mass or mound of just one flower in a single colour can have an amazing impact.

'When I am alone the flowers are really seen; I can pay attention to them. They are felt as presences.'

May Sarton, *Journal of a Solitude*

These rows of white flower heads and leaves in low clear Perspex boxes are the perfect complement to the graphic, contemporary style of this room. Three white dahlia heads, a few florets plucked from tall gladioli stems, and a collection of leaves with strong shapes and textures – nothing more, nothing less. Displaying flowers in unexpected ways enables one to appreciate them with new, more observant eyes. When white is seen on white, all the subtle variations in tone and texture are brought to the fore, with the fresh green of the leaves making an effective foil.

A mass of flowers but one dramatic statement: pink and red peonies and ranunculus heads floating in a sculptural red-lined bowl.

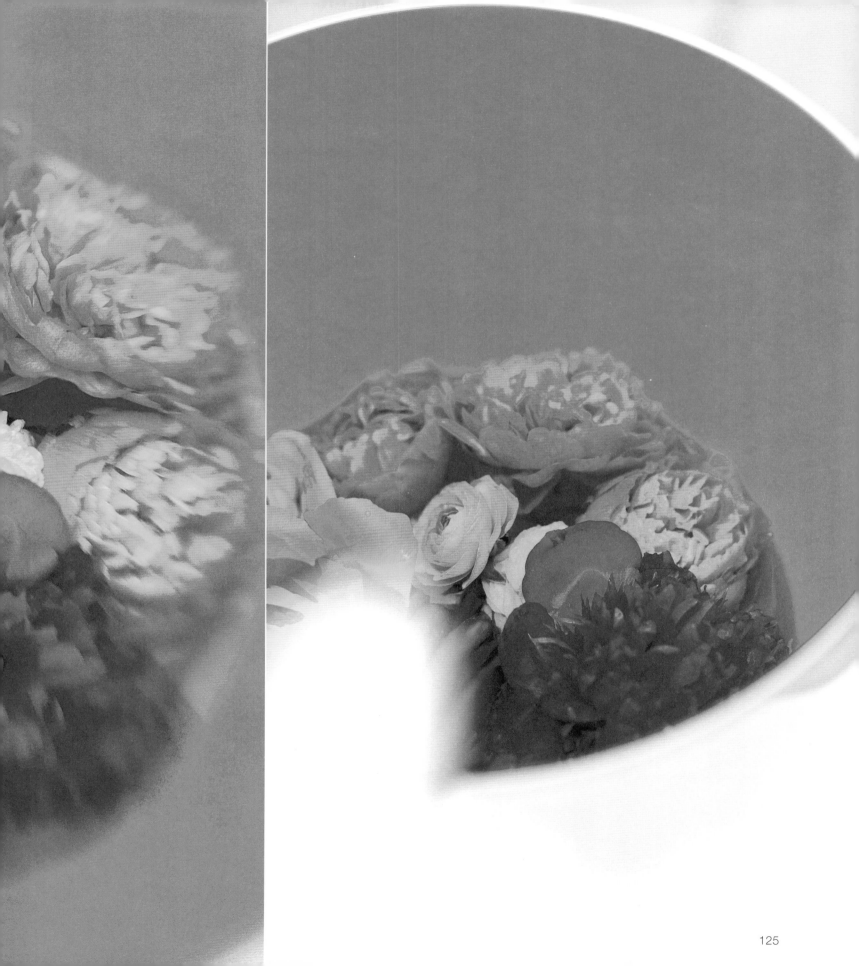

With the perfect partnership of bloom and container, you can sometimes afford to keep things very, very simple. Here, the purity and grace of white eucharis lilies is offset by a glass vase with scarlet lining. In such a pared-down arrangement, the milky green of the unopened buds and darker green of the stems take on extra significance. The fact that red and green are complementary colours only increases the impact – as can be seen in similar pairings in different white and red vases, some Perspex, some ceramic.

'Flowers can be cousins of the stars.'

Carl Sandburg, *There are Different Gardens*

Sculptural arrangements complement the colours and artworks in my green London kitchen. On the table, pink-and-white peonies, their heads heavy with the weight of their own petals, are lined up in a wedge-like glass vase – country garden flowers made modern by the minimalist container and lifted by wing-like leaves on either side. In a further unexpected and spontaneous touch, crimson-and-white petals of the striped rose, *Rosa mundi,* are laid in the boat-like hulls of coconut leaves.

'Even the sun-clouds this morning cannot manage such skirts.'

Sylvia Plath, *Poppies in October*

The markings on these oriental poppies are as striking as any Pop Art painting. In their natural state, the flower heads hang down and hide the raspberry-black blotches and beautiful central boss with its fringe of quivering black anthers. So, instead of displaying them as usual on longer stems, look these gorgeous flowers in the face by cutting the stems short and placing them in narrow-mouthed vases where they have no choice but to face upwards. No further ornament is necessary.

A bold colour scheme of black and yellow harks back to the 1950s and perfectly complements the mid-century modern table and the simple shapes of the ceramics. The tissue-paper whorls of ranunculus look as good massed in tiny posies as they do on arching graphic stems. Notice how each lemon-yellow petal is tinged with orange. Remove the pink camellia and the feeling would become even more minimalist.

Garden

For me, the garden is both a source of wonderful flowers and another space to decorate with them. Some of my favourite flowers – hellebores, with their dusky colours and shy, spotted faces; bluebells, fritillaries and tiny scented violets – are growing in my own garden, and I love to pick a few to bring into the house or arrange on a table outside. It is almost a cliché now to talk of the garden as an outdoor room, but how many people actually treat their garden as if that were the case, taking care to arrange tables, chairs and other outdoor furnishings, and decorating with fabric and flowers? We have looked at ways to transform the garden for a party, but little everyday touches, such as putting a freshly ironed cloth on a table, cushions on garden chairs, and arranging little bunches of flowers about the place, can make a commonplace corner into something truly delightful.

In this sunlit corner, tulips, bluebells and fritillaries from the garden are mixed with other flowers in soft pinks, mauves and maroons. The look is spontaneous and informal, using old milk bottles and jam jars which focus all attention on the flowers – milk bottles are also great for keeping stems in place in the wind. But the colour scheme is sophisticated, with lime-green guelder roses, viola and euphorbia leaves as a contrast, and the artful asymmetry of the arrangements has a quirky, uncommon charm.

'Wildflowers are perhaps the most enchanting... I love their delicacy, their disarming innocence, and their defiance of life itself.'

Grace Kelly

Snakeshead fritillaries can be found growing wild in flower meadows, but their chequerboard patterns in dark maroon and white have a sultry, sophisticated beauty and their shape, when seen in isolation against a clear coloured background, is surprisingly sculptural. Hellebores are another flower not often used for indoor arrangements, but their dusky colours and speckled faces also deserve to be studied at close hand. Displayed in simple vases that take only two or three blooms apiece, these flowers can be appreciated for the small living miracles that they are.

Sitting on a balcony off the sitting room, this small table filled with flowers draws the eye outdoors and helps to merge the house with the garden. The colours – single white peonies, with their golden-yellow anthers, lime-green alchemilla and a variegated hosta leaf – have been chosen to complement the impromptu striped fabric awning that has been thrown over the balcony. Simple modern glass and plastic containers in a variety of shapes and sizes echo the contemporary feeling inside the house.

'Flowers enable us to see like a butterfly.'

Dame Miriam Rothschild

Few people think of bringing wisteria indoors, but for those few short weeks when it's at its peak, why confine it to the garden where it is often only seen from far below? Bring armfuls of the pendulous blooms inside to hang in scented swags and drip elegantly from tall glass vases. The combination of pale mauve flowers and chartreuse foliage is show-stopping, while dark bearded iris are the perfect complement in terms of colour and strong sculptural shape.

151

Working with flowers

I cannot imagine living without flowers – the repeated rhythms of buying, conditioning, arranging and re-arranging them has become an integral part of my life. Like many other domestic tasks, this can be done quickly and efficiently, without a second thought. But I glean much more satisfaction from lingering over the different stages – from selecting the right blooms for the space and the season to choosing the best container to complement their shapes and colours – and I'm certain the extra time and effort shows in the results. Over the years, I've picked up tips on cutting and conditioning flowers from experts in the field and from my own experience, and am delighted to pass on this wisdom. Well-cared-for flowers not only look lovelier and last longer, they also enhance one's own experience of their brief beauty.

I find that flowers I've grown myself have a radiance and aura about them that is quite unlike those bought in the shops. If you have the space, grow your favourite flowers in abundance, so you won't feel bad about leaving a space in the border when you pick. Or set aside a small patch as a cutting garden. Once the preserve of large country houses, cutting gardens have become fashionable again, and the sight of row upon row of vibrant, brightly coloured flowers just waiting to be picked and arranged is always a joy.

154

Caring for flowers

One of the joys of living in London is being able to get up early and go to New Covent Garden Flower Market to buy armfuls of the freshest flowers straight from the stallholders – many of the flowers will have been growing in the ground just a few hours ago. Arriving home with all these treasures to decorate the house for a party feels so exciting. One feels like an artist with a new box of paints – the finished picture is not yet clear, but the colours and textures of the raw materials are so inspiring.

In the inevitable impatience to start arranging, it is important not to forget to care for the flowers properly. It's not just a matter of dumping them in water and waiting till they die – afford your flowers the respect they deserve and they will reward you with a far longer, more vibrant and beautiful life. Many will have come on long journeys – flown from faraway countries, packed in cardboard boxes and wrapped up in cellophane. Like human travellers, they will need refreshing on arrival. And all flowers, even if freshly picked from your own garden, should not be left for a minute without water. Any old buckets or large containers will do, and tall galvanized florist's buckets not only look good but also help support longer stems as they stand. Fill them one-third full with water – tepid is absorbed better than ice-cold. If you want to use flower food, now is the time to add it – the nutrients and anti-bacterial agents it contains can help the flowers cope with the unnatural conditions inside a house.

Conditioning flowers

Stems of shop-bought flowers should be re-cut at this stage – just the bottom few centimetres – and ideally at an angle so that they don't sit flat at the bottom of the bucket and have more of their centres exposed for water uptake. (Professional florists even do this underwater to avoid air locks forming in the capillary network of the stems.) Woody stems of trees and shrubs such as the sprays of blossom used on these pages should have the bottom few centimetres crushed with a hammer (this increases the area for

water uptake and prevents a seal forming). Be sure to use super-sharp scissors or secateurs for cutting to avoid causing unnecessary bruising or other damage.

Softer, sappy stems such as those of hellebores, poppies, ranunculus and euphorbia will benefit from being seared in boiling water – angle the flower heads to prevent them being scalded by the steam and dip the freshly-cut bases in three centimetres of water for a scant twenty seconds. Then place immediately in tepid water. Searing is worth trying on any flowers that always seem to droop when you try to arrange them inside, particularly garden flowers that have not been treated by florists. Roses and peonies will also benefit from searing, even if they have drooped already. Cut the stems at an angle first and they should pick up in an hour or two. If not, soak the entire stems and heads in a shallow bath of cold water.

The next important task is to remove all the lower leaves from the stems. No leaves should remain below the water line – while being conditioned or within the final arrangement – as they soon decay to form a bacterial soup that will not only smell but shorten the life of all of the flowers in that vase. Stripping the leaves also decreases the demands and stresses on newly cut flowers – leave enough to look attractive, and save the prettiest leaves for other purposes. Some can be added to other arrangements, or used to line clear vases for an unusual touch.

Ideally, the flowers should now be left in their buckets, in a cool place, out of direct sunlight, for a day or at least overnight. This may be more than your patience can bear, but it is definitely worth doing for a big party or wedding – the flowers will be beautifully vibrant and will last a good few days longer.

Arranging flowers

Preparing flowers in the above way can be a time-consuming job, but it is also a period during which to consider the different blooms and begin to formulate ideas. Place contrasting shapes and shades next to one another as you work – would the purple alliums, their

spheres of tiny flowers just opening, look better alongside crimson carnations or snowy white peonies? And might those deepest red-black ranunculus look best of all massed in a single bunch on their own? Keep any stray blossoms or buds that fall as you work – they can work great charm as part of very small-scale arrangements. It's a source of great satisfaction that so little is wasted – and anything unusable goes straight onto the compost heap.

Choosing containers is a crucial part of the fun of arranging flowers. Don't just go for the conventional option – as well as a huge collection of vases old and new, I keep pretty old jam jars and milk bottles, and also press drinking glasses, Moroccan tea glasses and vintage cups and saucers into use. Cast out the convention that tall stems go in tall vases and so on – rules are made to be broken, so experiment with your own ideas and let the flowers lead the way. It's really important to ensure that all your containers or glasses are absolutely clean before you start – even the smallest amount of bacteria will proliferate, with smelly and harmful consequences. Wash them thoroughly in hot soapy water before you use them. And once you have arranged your flowers, check the water levels every day, especially in hot weather – flowers can guzzle water extremely quickly and will wilt if levels get too low. Change the water altogether at least every other day, checking for spent flowers and leaves as you do so. Have an eye always on what could be re-used: if you are removing a delphinium spire because too many of the lower blooms have been lost, save the others for floating on water or showing off in small vases.

When beginning to arrange your flowers, really take time to look at the individual blooms and feel how they might be used to their best advantage. Again, go beyond the usual options: tall stems can look great, but there is nothing to stop you from cutting some of them short – sometimes a flower can be seen in a whole new light by displaying it in an unexpected way. Who says that the stems in a vase should all be roughly the same height? Why not leave some tall while others can peep over the rim like a floral ruff. In fact, who says flowers need stems at all? Some of the most original arrangements on these pages use the heads of flowers nipped off at the top of the stem and floated on water or threaded into garlands on lengths of cotton or fine fishing line.

New life for old

Thinking laterally like this is particularly useful when going through an arrangement that is several days old and is starting to fade. There will be plenty of good blooms that can be given new life in a different arrangement – gladioli florets can be plucked off the stems, and the small sprays of buds that sprout from the main stems of delphiniums can be used in new ways. It is also a way of redeeming bouquets sent as presents where far too many types of flowers in too many colours have been crammed together with little thought or artistry. Take time to separate out the different types of flowers, perhaps pairing them with others from your own garden or elsewhere. It's hard to think of any flower that isn't beautiful when used in the right way. Some people do not like carnations, for instance – but they come in stunning colours, including white with a raspberry ripple picotee edge, and are incredibly long lasting. I love to weave them into garlands – they look great with that other fashion outcast, the French marigold – or float the heads in water. Splitting the calyx that holds the petals tightly in place can give a softer look to the flower heads.

Foliage is another area where too much tradition holds sway. Flowers don't have to be teamed with their own natural leaves. Dahlias, for instance, have unremarkable foliage and look far smarter with a few perky lupin leaves. Hydrangea heads look better on their own, but the large textural leaves are good for lining clear vases. And puckered scrolling hosta leaves, or fresh green spears of violas, can give a lift to almost any arrangement.

When you finally come to the end of the road, and it's time to get rid of your flowers, try not to throw them away. Rose petals can be strewn on lawns or on the surface of ponds, or dried in the traditional way to make pot pourri. And as for any other remains, just put them on the compost heap. In one more satisfying turn of the cycle, they will decay into soil that will one day grow flowers of its own.

Designers Guild Stockists

Designers Guild fabric, wallpaper, furniture and accessories are available from the Designers Guild Showroom and Homestore, 267-277 Kings Road, London SW3 5EN, tel 020 7351 5775, and also from selected retailers including:

Bath & N.E.Somerset

ROSSITERS OF BATH
38-41 Broad Street Bath BA1 5LP
01225 462227 / 01225 444160 (f)
rossbath@globalnet.co.uk

Berkshire

JACQUELINE INTERIORS
18 Brockenhurst Road South Ascot SL5 9DL
01344 638867
jackie@jackieinteriors.fsnet.co.uk

Buckinghamshire

JOHN LEWIS FURNISHINGS & LEISURE
Holmers Farm Way Cressex Centre
High Wycombe HP12 4NW 01494 462666

MORGAN GILDER FURNISHINGS
14 High Street Stony Stratford
Milton Keynes MK11 1AF 01908 568674

Cheshire

JOHN LEWIS
Wilmslow Road Cheadle SK8 3BZ
01614 914914

Cornwall

CASA FINA INTERIORS
29 River Street Truro TR1 2SJ 01872 270818
mail@casa-fina.co.uk www.casa-fina.co.uk

Essex

CLEMENT JOSCELYNE
9-11 High Street Brentwood CM14 4RG
01277 225420 info@clementjoscelyne.co.uk

LOTTIE MUTTON
45 King Street Saffron Walden CB11 1EU
01799 522 252 lottiemutton@aol.com

Gloucestershire

UPSTAIRS DOWNSTAIRS
19 Rotunda Terrace Montpellier Street
Cheltenham GL59 1SW 01242 514023
homeclimatesltd@btinternet.com

Hampshire

CLARKES BLINDS
25 Farnborough Street Farnborough GU14 8AG
01252 544 568 / 01252 375 607 (f)
info@clarkesblinds.co.uk
67a Crookham Road Fleet GU51 5DT
01252 628263 info@clarkesblinds.co.uk

DESIGN HOUSE
7 Great Minster Street
Winchester SO23 9HA 01962 840 949
designhousewinchester@btinternet.com

THE INTERIOR TRADING CO
55-57 Marmion Road Southsea PO5 2AT
023 9283 8038 enquiries@interior-trading.co.uk

Hertfordshire

CLEMENT JOSCELYNE
Market Square Bishop's Stortford CM23 3XA
01279 713010 info@clementjoscelyne.co.uk
111-112 Bancroft Hitchin SG5 1LT
01462 436533 info@clementjoscelyne.co.uk

DAVID LISTER INTERIORS
6 Leyton Road Harpenden AL5 2TL
01582 764270

ELIZABETH STEWART
DESIGN & FURNISHING
201-203 High Street Potters Bar EN6 5DA
01707 663433 esdesign@ukf.net
1 Exchange Buildings High Street
Barnet EN5 5SY
020 8440 6363 esb@elizabethstewart.co.uk

Kent

FABRICS IN CANTERBURY
Albert House 14 St Johns Lane Castle Street
Canterbury CT1 2QG 01227 457555
fabricsincant@aol.com

JOHN LEWIS
Bluewater Greenhithe DA9 9SA 01322 624123

KOTIKI INTERIORS LTD
22-24 Grove Hill Road
Tunbridge Wells TN1 1RZ
01892 521369 kotikiinteriors@aol.com

MARY ENSOR INTERIORS
13 Crescent Road Tunbridge Wells TN1 2LU
01892 523003 interiors@maryensor.co.uk

Lancashire

ASHLEIGH INTERIORS
146 Main Street Warton Nr Carnforth LA5 9PJ
01524 735454 ashleigh-interiors@tiscali.co.uk
www.ashleighinteriors.co.uk

JOHN THOMPSON DESIGN CENTRE
336 Church Street Blackpool FY1 3QH
01253 302515

Leicestershire

BARKERS INTERIORS
94 Main Street Woodhouse Eaves
Loughborough LE12 8RZ 01509 890473
barkerid@aol.com

ELIZABETH STANHOPE INTERIORS
27 Mill Street Oakham Rutland LE15 6EA
01572 722345 / 01572 722616 (f)
showroom@elizabethstanhope.co.uk

HARLEQUIN INTERIORS
11 Loseby Lane Leicester LE1 5DR
0116 262 0994 harlequinint@aol.com

INDIGO ACRE
4 Castle Gate House Bath Street
Ashby de la Zouch LE65 2FH
01530 411744 / 01530 560260 (f)
yvonne@indigoacre.co.uk

Lincolnshire

UNION INTERIORS
Union Street Grantham NG31 6NZ
01476 593388 enquires@uniongrantham.com

London

CAMERON BROOM
The Courtyard 15 Bellevue Road SW17 7EG
020 8767 2241
triciacameron@cameronbroom.com

CHARLES PAGE INTERIORS LTD
61 Fairfax Road NW6 4EE 020 7328 9851
info@charlespage.co.uk

DESIGNERS GUILD
267 & 277 Kings Road SW3 5EN
020 7351 5775 showroom@designersguild.com

HARRODS
87-135 Brompton Road
Knightsbridge SW1X 7XL 020 7730 1234

HEAL & SON
196 Tottenham Court Road W1P 9LD
020 7636 1666

INTERIORS OF CHISWICK
454 Chiswick High Road W4 5TT
020 8994 0073
enquiries@interiorsofchiswick.co.uk

JOHN LEWIS
Oxford Street W1A 1EX
020 7629 7711

LIBERTY
Regent Street W1 6AH 020 7734 1234
interiorstyling@liberty.co.uk www.liberty.co.uk

PETER JONES
Sloane Square SW1W 8EL 020 7730 3434

REVAMP INTERIORS
26 Knights Hill West Norwood SE27 0HY
020 8670 5151 / 020 8766 8500 (f)
revampint@aol.com www.revampinteriors.com

SELFRIDGES
Oxford Street W1A 1AB 020 7629 1234

Manchester

HEALS
11 New Cathedral Street Manchester M1 1AD
0161 819 3000

Merseyside

ELAINE CUNNINGHAM INTERIORS
392 Aigburth Road Aigburth
Liverpool L19 3QD 0845 612 6600
enquires@elainecunninghaminteriors.co.uk

Norfolk

DESIGNERS GUILD AT THE GRANARY
5 Bedford Street Norwich NR2 1AL
01603 623220
info@clementjoscelyne.co.uk

Nottinghamshire

NASH INTERIORS
60 Derby Road Nottingham NG1 5FD
0115 941 3811
interiors@nash-interiors.com

Oxfordshire

FAIRFAX INTERIORS
The Old Bakery High Street Lower Brailes
Nr Banbury OX15 5HW 01608 685301
caroline.elliott@btconnect.com

STELLA MANNERING LTD
2 Woodstock Road Oxford OX2 6HT
01865 557196
stella@stellamanneringltd.co.uk

Somerset

PAUL CARTER
The Studio Elm House Chip Lane
Taunton TA1 1BZ 01823 330404
thestudio@paulcarter.co.uk

THE CURTAIN POLE
64 High Street Glastonbury BA6 9DY
01458 834166 curpole@yahoo.co.uk

Staffordshire
THE WILLIAM MORRIS SHOP
11 & 12 Berkley Court Brunswick Street
Newcastle-under-Lyme ST5 1TT 01782 619772

Suffolk
CLEMENT JOSCELYNE
16 Langton Place Bury St Edmunds IP33 1NE
01284 753824 info@clementjoscelyne.co.uk

EDWARDS OF HADLEIGH
53 High Street Hadleigh IP7 5AB
01473 827271 info@edwardsonline.co.uk

FANNY & FRANK
8 Market Hill Woodbridge IP12 4LU
01394 380435 theteam@fannyandfrank.com

Surrey
BABAYAN PEARCE INTERIORS
Braeside House High Street Oxshott KT22 0JP
01372 842437

CHAMELEON
7 High Street Esher KT10 9RL 01372 470720
veronica@chameleonhomes.com
83 Queens Road Weybridge KT13 9UQ
01932 874966 / 01932 848 194 (f)

CREATIVE INTERIORS
20 Chipstead Station Parade
Chipstead CR5 3TE 01737 555443

GORGEOUS
19 Bell Street Reigate Surrey RH2 7AD
01737 2228461 / 01737 222846 (f)

HEAL & SON
Tunsgate Guildford GU1 3QU 01483 576715
49-51 Eden Street Kingston upon Thames
KT1 1BW 020 8614 5900

JOHN LEWIS
Wood Street Kingston upon Thames KT1 1TE
020 8547 3000

J DECOR INTERIORS
3 South Street Epsom KT18 7PJ
01372 721773 jdecor@btconnect.com

PEPPERSTITCH DESIGNS LTD
198 High Street Egham Surrey TW20 9ED
01784 430501 pepperstitch1@aol.com

SABLE INTERIORS
7 Criterion Buildings Portsmouth Road
Thames Ditton KT7 0ST 020 8398 7779

SAGE
High Street Ripley GU23 6BB 01483 224396
howard@hsage.freeserve.co.uk

Sussex
CORNFIELD HOUSE
32-34 Cornfield Rd Eastbourne
East Sussex BN21 4QH 01323 727193

MARY ENSOR INTERIORS
37 High Street Frant
Nr Tunbridge Wells TN3 9DT 01892 750101
interiors@maryensor.co.uk

MISTER SMITH INTERIORS
1-3 The Parade Croft Road Crowborough
East Sussex TN6 1DR 01892 664152
info@mistersmith.co.uk
www.mistersmith.co.uk
23 New Road Brighton East Sussex BN1 1UF
01273 605574 info@mistersmith.co.uk
www.mistersmith.co.uk

SUTTONS FURNISHINGS
56 Church Road Brighton & Hove
East Sussex BN3 2FP 01273 723728

West Midlands
JOHN CHARLES INTERIORS
349 Hagley Road Edgbaston
Birmingham B17 8DN 0121 420 3977

JOHN LEWIS
Touchwood Solihull B91 3RA 0121 704 1121

MARY BARBER FRAY INTERIOR DESIGN
The Coppice 23 Plymouth Rd Barnt Green
Birmingham B45 8JF 0121 445 6500
mary@marybarberfray.co.uk

Worcestershire
CLOUD NINE INTERIORS
12 St Andrews Street Droitwich Spa WR9 8DY
01905 779988 cloud9interiors@hotmail.com

Yorkshire
CEDAR HOUSE INTERIORS
Home Farm Mill Lane Stillington
York YO61 1NG 01347 811 813
cedarhsint@aol.com

HOMEWORKS
Charles House 4 Castlegate Tickhill
Doncaster DN11 9QU 01302 743978
interiors@homeworks-tickhill.co.uk

JAMES BRINDLEY OF HARROGATE
29-31 James Street Harrogate HG1 1QY
01423 560757 enquiries@jamesbrindley.com

MADELAINE PEACE INTERIORS LTD
145 Oakbrook Road Sheffield S11 7EB
0114 230 6666

Northern Ireland
BEAUFORT INTERIORS LTD
597-599 Lisburn Road Belfast BT9 7GS
102-106 Main Street Moria BT67 0LH
02892 2619508 / 02892 612765 (f)
info@beaufortinteriors.co.uk

FULTONS FINE FURNISHINGS
Hawthorne House Boucher Crescent
Belfast BT12 6HU 0870 600 0186
The Point Derrychara Enniskillen BT74 6JF
01365 323739
55-63 Queen Street Lurgan BT66 8BN
01762 314980

MOCHA DESIGN
21-23 Spencer Road Londonderry
Co. Londonderry BT47 6AA 028 7131 1900

Scotland
CATHERINE HENDERSON
10 Kildrostan Street Pollokshields
Glasgow G41 4LU 0141 423 4321
catherine@catherinehenderson.com

CHELSEA MCLAINE INTERIOR DESIGN
161 Milngavie Road Bearsden
Glasgow G61 3DY 0141 942 2833
margot@chelseamclaine.freeserve.co.uk

DESIGNWORKS
38 Gibson Street Glasgow G12 8NX
0141 339 9520
info@designworks-scotland.co.uk

INNOV8 INTERIORS
1 Ainslie Street West Pitkerro Industrial Estate
Broughty Ferry Dundee DD5 3RR
01382 477000 design@innov8interiors.co.uk
www.innov8interiors.co.uk

JEFFREYS INTERIORS
8 North West Circus Place Edinburgh EH3 6ST
0845 8822 655 / 0845 8822 656 (f)
jeff@jeffreys-interiors.co.uk

JOHN LEWIS
St James Centre Edinburgh EH1 3SP
0131 556 9121
Buchanan Galleries Glasgow G1 2GF
0141 353 6677

LAURA GILL DESIGN LTD
38 High Street Dunblane FK15 0AD
01786 821948 lauragill@talk21.com

SHAPES
1 Bankhead Medway Sighthill Edinburgh EH11 4BY
0131 4533222 / 0131 4536444 (f)
sales@shapesfurniture.co.uk

Wales
TAYLOR'S ETC
143 Colchester Avenue Cardiff S. Glamorgan
CF23 7UZ 029 20 358400 / 01792 791103 (f)

Eire
BRIAN S. NOLAN LTD
102 Upper Georges Street Dun Laoghaire
Co. Dublin 01 2800564

D&D COLEMAN INTERIOR DESIGN
Dyann House Donadea Co. Kildare
045 893010

J LYONS INTERIORS
Market House The Square
Castlerea Co. Roscommon
094 9620339 / 094 9620788 (f)

O'MAHONY INTERIORS
Enniskeane West Cork 023 47123
o'mahonyinteriors@eircom.net

ORMOND SOFT FURNISHINGS
Barrack Lane Carrick-on-Suir
Co. Tipperary 051 640857
Ballinakill Shopping Centre Dumore Road
Waterford Co. Tipperary 051 820830
Castle Court Castle Road Oran
Co. Galway 09 1792210
design@ormondsoftfurnishings.com

THE WHYTE HOUSE
Market Lane Westport County Mayo
09 850891 whytek@eircom.net

WILDTHINGS
Main Street Celbridge Co. Kildare
01 6274977 Main Street Enfield Co. Meath
046 9549200 wildthingsshop@eircom.net

WINDOW ATTIRE
Mill Road Ennis Co. Clare 065 6823866
windowattire@eircom.net

Designers Guild products are available in over 60 countries; for further information please contact our London head office on 020 7893 7400 or info@designersguild.com or visit our website www.designersguild.com. For Australia please contact Radford Furnishings, tel 03 9552 6000, and for New Zealand please contact Icon Textiles, tel 04 474 1076.

DESIGNERS GUILD is a registered trademark of Designers Guild Ltd.

Acknowledgements

Thank you again to our very special team
as we work together to create another book:
Anne Furniss, Meryl Lloyd, James Merrell,
Elspeth Thompson and my very talented creative
stylist Liza Giles.

To the team at Designers Guild for their energy
and support without whom this book would not be
possible, especially: Amanda Back, Helen Burke,
Anna Crickmore, Blythe Evans, Lydia Hargrave,
Claire Herbert, Ciara O'Flanagan, Liz Poole.

Also thanks to Lucy Merrell, Richard Polo, Marissa Tuazon.

All photographs by James Merrell except pages 22/23, 78/79, 102/103,
140/141, 154/155, 156/157 (1,6,8,9), 158/159 (1,2,3,5,6) by Tricia Guild

Quote page 70: © Alice Walker 'Revolutionary Petunias and Other Poems'
(New York: Harcourt Brace Jovanovich 1973).

First published in 2008 by Quadrille Publishing Limited
Alhambra House, 27–31 Charing Cross Road, London WC2H OLS

Project editor Anne Furniss
Design Meryl Lloyd
Tricia Guild's creative stylist Liza Giles
Production Ruth Deary, Vincent Smith
Typesetting and artwork Keith Holmes redbus

British Library Cataloguing in Publication Data
A catalogue record for this book is available from the British Library
ISBN (978) 1 84400 520 8

Printed and bound in China
10 9 8 7 6 5 4 3 2 1